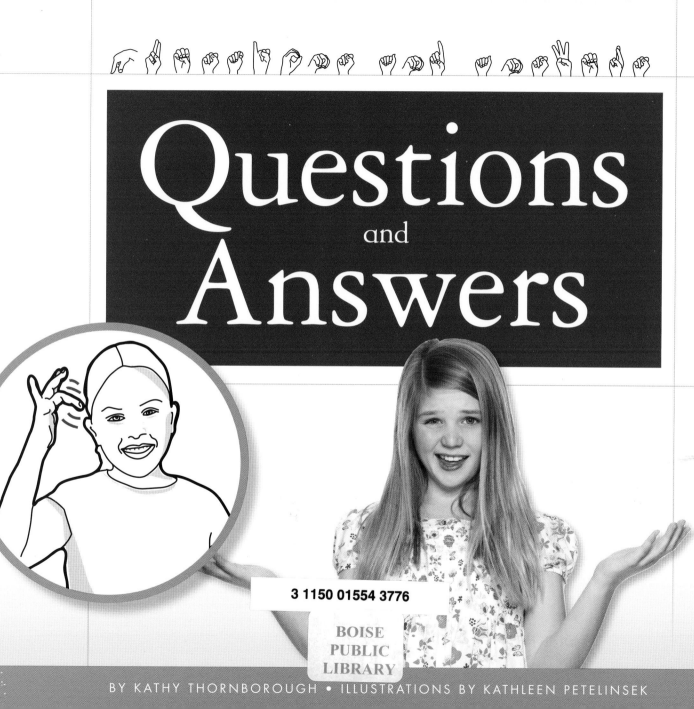

Questions
and
Answers

BY KATHY THORNBOROUGH • ILLUSTRATIONS BY KATHLEEN PETELINSEK

The Child's World®

PUBLISHED by The Child's World®
1980 Lookout Drive • Mankato, MN 56003-1705
800-599-READ • www.childsworld.com

ACKNOWLEDGMENTS
The Child's World®: Mary Berendes, Publishing Director
The Design Lab: Design
Jody Jensen Shaffer: Editing

PHOTO CREDITS
© Boris Ryaposov/Shutterstock.com: 7; Coprid/Shutterstock.
com: 22; dean bertoncelj/Shutterstock.com: 11; g-stockstudio/
Shutterstock.com: 13; huronphoto/iStock.com: 14; joxxxxjo/
iStock.com: 9; LCBallard/iStock.com: 21; maxkabakov/iStock.
com: 10; Mr_Khan/iStock.com: 18; PathDoc/Shutterstock.com:
4; perkmeup/iStock.com: 6; Ramona Heim/Shutterstock.com:
cover, 1, 23; osliothman/iStock.com: back cover, 3; sanneberg/
Shutterstock.com: 19; shipfactory/Shutterstock.com: 15; tmcnem/
iStock.com: 8; Vlue/Shutterstock.com: 5; Yuangkratoke Nakhorn/
Shutterstock.com: 15; zimmytws/Shutterstock.com: 12; zoom-
zoom/iStock.com: 20

ISBN 9781626873216
LCCN 2014934492

PRINTED in the United States of America
Mankato, MN
July 2014
PA02216

A SPECIAL THANKS TO OUR ADVISERS:

As a member of a deaf family that spans four generations, Kim Bianco Majeri lives, works, and plays amongst the deaf community.

Carmine L. Vozzolo is an educator of children who are deaf and hard of hearing, as well as their families.

NOTE TO PARENTS AND EDUCATORS:

The understanding of any language begins with the acquisition of vocabulary, whether the language is spoken or manual. The books in the Talking Hands series provide readers, both young and old, with a first introduction to basic American Sign Language signs. Combining close photocues and simple, but detailed, line illustrations, children and adults alike can begin the process of learning American Sign Language. Let these books be an introduction to the world of American Sign Language. Most languages have regional dialects and multiple ways of expressing the same thought. This is also true for sign language. We have attempted to use the most common version of the signs for the words in this series. As with any language, the best way to learn is to be taught in person by a frequent user. It is our hope that this series will pique your interest in sign language.

Question

Draw a question mark in the air.
(It will look backward to the
person you are speaking to.)

**"Question" in Spanish
is "pregunta."**

3

Answer

"Answer" in German is "antwort."

What?

Shrug your shoulders and move your hands slightly from side to side.

Who?

Curl and wiggle your right
index finger near your mouth.

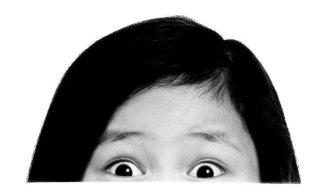

"Who?" in Japanese
is "Dare?"

Move your right index finger
in a circle around your
left index finger.

Tapping your watch and
shrugging your shoulders
can make this sign, too.

Yesterday

Make a fist with your right hand and point your thumb up. Starting with your thumb near your chin, move it up toward your ear.

"Yesterday" in Spanish is "ayer."

YESTERDAY

AM

PM

Today

Make the "Y" shape, but face
your hands toward you.
Motion downward twice.

Tomorrow

Make a fist with your right hand and point your thumb up. With your hand near your right cheek, move it down and away.

"Tomorrow" in French is "demain."

Where?

Point your right index finger upward.
Then wiggle your wrist slightly
from left to right.

"Where?" in Japanese
is "Doko?"

Here

Face both flat hands upward.
Then move them in flat circles twice.

"Here" in Spanish
is "aquí."

You Are Here

There

Point away from you.

"There" in German is "da."

Can I?

Make the "S" sign with both hands.
Move both hands downward.
Then point to yourself.

"Can I?" is sometimes switched with "May I?"

Will you?

"Will you?"
in French is
"Voulez-vous?"

Your flat right hand moves from your face outward. Then point to the person you are speaking to.

Yes

Make the "S" sign with your right hand. Move your wrist downward a few times while nodding your head "yes."

Pointing your thumbs up means something is good.

"No" means the same thing in many languages.

No

Touch the middle and index fingers of your right hand to your thumb while shaking your head "no."

Put the backs of your hands together, with your fingers touching. Then roll your hands so your fingers point up.

"How?" in Spanish is "¿Cómo?"

How many?

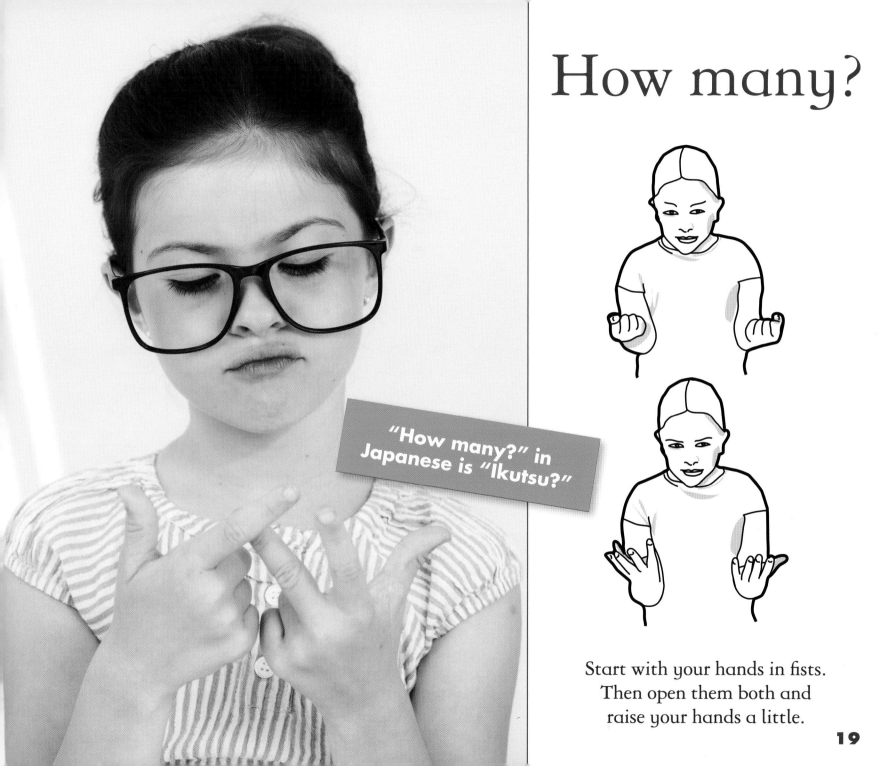

"How many?" in Japanese is "Ikutsu?"

Start with your hands in fists.
Then open them both and
raise your hands a little.

19

All

Spell A-L-L with your fingers.

"All" in German is "alle."

Some

Slice your right hand
over your flat left hand.
Pretend you are slicing a pie.

**"Some" in French
is "certains."**

None

Both of your hands make the "O" sign. Move your hands forward quickly while shaking your head "no."

"None" in Japanese is "nashi."

Why?

With your hand facing your face, wiggle your right middle finger a few times.

"Why?" in Spanish is "¿Por qué?"

23

A SPECIAL THANK YOU!

A special thank you to our models from the Program for Children Who are Deaf and Hard of Hearing at the Alexander Graham Bell Elementary School in Chicago, Illinois.

Alina's favorite things to do are art, soccer, and swimming. DJ is her brother!

Dareous likes football. His favorite team is the Detroit Lions. He also likes to play video games.

Darionna likes the swings and merry-go-round on the playground. She also loves art.

DJ loves playing the harmonica and video games. Alina is his sister!

Jasmine likes writing and math in school. She also loves to swim.

24

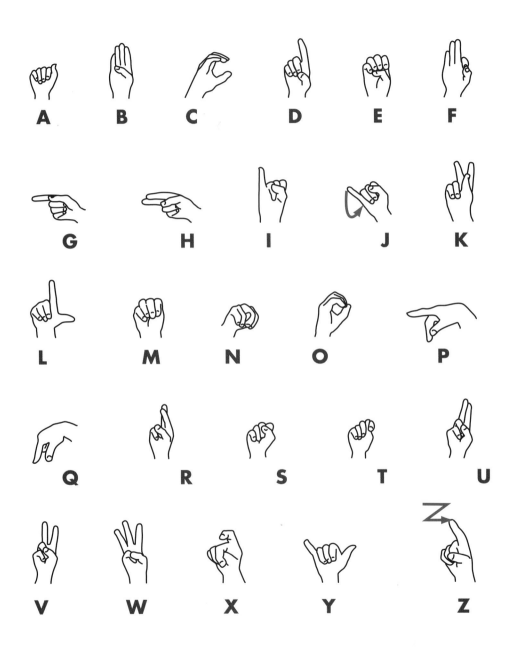